P9-BID-385

Journal
ME!

A Pocketbook for Girls

Helen Raica-Klotz

Resource Publications, Inc.
San Jose, California

Reprint Department
Resource Publications, Inc.
160 E. Virginia Street #290
San Jose, CA 95112-5876
1-408-286-8505 (voice)
1-408-287-8748 (fax)

ISBN 0-89390-449-X

Printed in the United States of America

03 02 01 00 99 | 5 4 3 2 1

Editorial director: Nick Wagner
Acquisition editor: Kenneth Guentert
Prepress manager: Elizabeth J. Asborno
Production coordinator: Mike Sagara
Copyeditor: Robin Witkin

*This book is dedicated
to my children,
Gaia and Gabriel,
who have reawakened
the power of my words
through their love.*

Contents

Note to Group Facilitators . . . . *vii*
Introduction. 1
The Journal. 7

Section One: ME

Connections 11
Future. 17
Feelings 23
Self. 29
Girls and Boys 37
Masks 43

Section Two: ME and Others

Family 51
Support Systems 57
Anger. 63
Boundaries 69
Saying No 75
Me, Special Me 81

Bibliography 87

Note To
Group Facilitators

This book is designed to inspire your young women to start discovering more about themselves: who they are; what they value; what their dreams, and fears, may be. This book is written with the belief that only when we truly know ourselves can we truly love who we are.

I would like to think that the girls who write in these pages will discover the power writing holds for self-discovery. I hope that they will return to these questions again and again, discovering new answers and new truths throughout their adolescence. I believe, with your encouragement, these things are possible.

Because these journals are private, the young women should not be forced to share their writings with the rest of the group, or with anyone at all. We know that journal writing is only effective if the audience disappears and the only person you write for is you and you alone. However, you may discover that, through their excitement at learning more about themselves, the group is willing to share ideas and words that they have written. This is a wonderful thing.

I hope that you will encourage your group to make use of this journal book and that you, as the group facilitator, will use it as well. Although the answers may change as we get older, many of the questions women face in our society remain the same.

Welcome. Welcome to the wonderful and magical world of journaling.

Introduction

Welcome

Welcome to your journal. Although this little book may not seem like a big deal (and it isn't), the writing that you put inside these pages is. Because writing is a magical way to discover all sorts of things about yourself and your ideas. And that is a big deal.

The Rules

I have only two rules for this journal that I hope you can keep. My Number-One Rule is: This is *your writing*, meant to be read by you alone. Unless you're really comfortable doing so, there is no need to share what you write here with anyone else—your parents, your teacher, your best friends, your brothers or sisters. No one has to read what you write in these pages but you. This way you don't have to worry about what other people will think of *what you write* (because they'll never see it anyway), so the only thing left to worry about is *what to write*. Of course, you can share ideas that you get from this journal with other people, but I think the actual words should be for you alone. So keep this book in a safe place—one where people can't run across it and read it by "mistake."

My Number-Two Rule is: There is no right or wrong answer to any of these questions. If you answer the question or write about something totally different; if you draw your answer instead of using words; if your writing is filled with spelling errors and messy handwriting (like my journal)—all of this is OK. This is your book; the questions and ideas for writing that I give you are simply here to help you out. But you decide what questions work for you and what exercises are effective. And you decide how you are going to answer these questions for yourself.

Why Journal?

So what's the point of this journal? Well, as I said before, journaling helps in self-discovery, by keeping a record of your thoughts, feelings, opinions, hopes, fears, and beliefs. And this is important stuff to know. Almost every decision we make in life, from whether to eat waffles or Raisin Bran for breakfast to whether or not to go to college, is based on what we know and on how well we know ourselves.

Journal writing can also help you become more creative, by making you express yourself in concrete words. You may discover poems, music, songs, drawings, and short stories waiting for you in the blank pages of this book—expressions that you already have inside you but never had the chance to release before.

Journals can also be great emotional therapy. Sometimes you can feel better by writing about things that bother you. Sometimes journals can help you decide exactly what your feelings are and give you ideas about what you can do with these feelings.

A journal can also serve as a history of where you were and what you were feeling at the age you are now. Think about it: You will never be where you are, at this time, again. That's important enough to keep some kind of record of, don't you think? After all, not only dead presidents and war heroes should have their own history books—you should, too.

Suggestions

Try writing in your journal every day. That may seem like a lot at first, but once you get used to it, it becomes a habit, like brushing your teeth in the morning or putting on your pj's at night. Easy stuff.

I suggest you journal for ten minutes on every question. Oh, and remember to record the date, and even the place where you are writing, every time you make a journal entry. It makes reading old journals a lot more fun and insightful.

Now, if your words fill up more than the space we've given you, find some more paper and keep writing! Some girls choose to pick out their own journal book, decorating their own cover, picking out the paper, and even creating a special box to keep it in. The important thing is that they found a book filled with blank pages so they can write as much as they want—not only about my questions but about anything else they would like to explore. A lot of girls also use it to draw in, put pictures in, make top-ten lists in, and so on. Feel free to be creative!

But write. And don't be scared. Mina Shaughnessy, author of *Errors and Expectations: A Guide for the Teacher of Basic Writing*, said, "Writing is something writers are always learning to do." I think that's true. No one, including me, writes wonderful ideas and great sentences every single time. And yes, there are some days you may have "writer's block" and can't think of anything to say. So if you are new to journaling, and a little uncomfortable, or if you've tried to write and been "blocked," here are some techniques you can use.

Techniques

There are different ways to write in your journal, and I've listed a few for you to try. I encourage you to play with each of these techniques at least once, and keep the ones that work for you. You may decide to use one or two favorites, or you may decide that all of them work for you—or that none do. If that happens, create your own! But here's a place to begin.

1. Freewriting

Read the question, and then put your pen to the paper and write everything, everything, that comes into your mind for ten minutes. Even if it doesn't make sense, or it's disorganized, don't stop writing. And don't worry about your handwriting, or spelling, or grammar (this is a journal, remember?). The idea is that if you keep writing, your mind will get rid of all the junk

thoughts and get into your real ideas. And
sometimes you even find yourself writing stuff
you didn't even know existed!

*This is a great exercise for those of us who
have been criticized for our writing, grammar,
and spelling and who find the idea of writing
anything down on paper rather scary.*

2. Looped Freewriting
After freewriting for ten minutes, go back and
underline one part you want to explore further.
Copy that part on the top of a fresh page. Write
for another ten minutes about everything that
comes to mind about this topic or until you run
out of things to say.

*If you have the time, this is usually effective
because it forces you to write after you've
cleared your head, and you can really focus on
the questions.*

3. Distancing
Pretend to write about yourself as a character in
a book or as a good friend. So rather than using
"I" and "me" to talk about yourself and your
feelings, use "she." For example, "She felt angry
that her parents wouldn't let her go out past
eleven o'clock."

*Sometimes the distance this gives can allow
you to see yourself more honestly.*

4. **Dialoguing**

Create someone to talk to, and have that person talk back. Write out a conversation that looks similar to a script of a play, where you carry on a discussion with someone else, anyone you choose. Think about it: you could talk to your cat, the Statue of Liberty, or Alanis Morrisette. One girl even created "Ms. J": yup, her journal.

It's nice to hear a point of view different than your own. And it's great for the imagination!

5. **Mapping**

Write your first idea in a circle in the middle of the page. Put additional ideas in circles around the first circle, using lines to connect them with one another. When you finish, all your ideas will be connected in a "map," showing where your ideas started and where they ended up. I often use different colored markers to show a clearer connection between ideas.

This gives a nice flowchart for ideas and works well when you have a lot of things to say but aren't sure where to begin. This is also nice for us visual learners, who like to see things laid out in front of us.

The Journal

Beginning

Here you go!

The journaling questions are divided into two sections: ME, and ME and Others. As you might have guessed, the first section deals with questions about you, and the second section deals with questions about your relationships with other people—your friends, your family, and others. Each section has six subtopics, with five questions in each subtopic.

So here you have a list of sixty questions. Some are serious, some are focused, and some are just for fun. Some ask you to draw, to paste in pictures, to make lists. All ask you to put your pen to the paper. I hope you use them to discover new truths and new questions for yourself. Good luck, and good writing.

Section One

ME

Connections

1.
What is your idea of the perfect date?

2.

Tell the children's story you heard most often growing up.

3.

Describe the weirdest dream you ever had.

4.
What's your favorite movie? Why?

5.

If you were told you had twenty-four hours left to live, what would you want to do during that time?

Future

6.

If you could describe yourself in ten years, what would you be doing? Where would you be living? Who would surround you?

7.

What are the places you would love to visit? Draw or put pictures of these places below, and describe them.

8.

If you had a daughter and could give her three gifts, what would they be?

9.
What do you want to "be" when you grow up? Why?

10.

Imagine you are ninety years old and you are describing your life experiences to someone. What would you have to say?

Feelings

11.

Write down the lyrics of your favorite song. What do they mean to you?

12.
What do you wish you knew about being in love that no one ever told you?

13.
What does laughter feel like?

14.

**If you could build a memorial
to all the losses you have had in
your life, what would it look like?**

15.

What would your life be like
if you had no emotions?

Self

16.

**Describe your perfect body and face.
What do you wish you looked like?
When you are done describing this
"perfect person," write about where this
image comes from. (Where have you seen
a person who looks like this, and who
thinks she is attractive?)**

17.

What do you do to make yourself more attractive (hair, makeup, clothing)? Why do you do it?

18.

Find a picture of yourself as a child, age six or seven. Then find a picture of yourself now. Describe each person as if you've never seen her before. What do they (you) look like?

19.

Go to a mirror and look at yourself without putting on any makeup or doing your hair. Set a timer for three minutes. Look carefully at yourself for those three minutes and say the words, "I *(your name here)* am a beautiful woman. I love the way I look, and my face and body make me very happy." Repeat this phrase for the entire three minutes. When the time is up, write about how you felt about the exercise.

20.
Write about a characteristic you've inherited from your mother or from another woman in your family.

Girls and Boys

21.

Imagine that you were born a boy instead of a girl. How would your life be different?

22.
What is a "feminist"?

23.

What are three things you would love to ask a boy but would never dare ask?

24.
Do you act differently around boys than you do around girls? Why?

25.

Describe the perfect world in which to be a woman and in which to be a girl.

Masks

26.

Draw a picture of yourself—who you really are. Now draw a picture of what the rest of the world (school, parents, coaches) sees. What is the difference between the two pictures?

27.
Who knows who you really are, deep down?

28.

If you had to choose three objects (not people) that would sum up who you are, what would they be?

29.
**Do girls wear different "masks"
than boys? Are they expected to act a
certain way because they are girls?**

30.

**Describe a time when you
pretended to be someone or something
you aren't. How did it feel?**

Section Two

ME And Others

Family

31.

If your family was a color, what color would they be and why? An animal? A type of music?

32.
**Describe your parents' relationship
with each other. Would you like
to have a relationship like theirs?**

33.
What's the biggest thing adults don't understand about teenagers?

34.

Name one thing that you love about your family. Now name one thing you would like to change.

35.
**Write down in large letters
"I am *(your name here)*,
daughter of *(your mother's name)*,
granddaughter of *(grandmother's
full name)*."
Say these words out loud.
Write about how you feel saying
these words.**

Support Systems

36.

**In one column, list all the people
you love. In another column, list all the
people who love you. Now draw a big
heart around everyone you listed and
write a Valentine to all of them
(even if it's not February!).**

37.
Describe your closest friends.
How did you meet? When did you decide to become friends?

38.
Do you believe in God?

39.
Fill in the blanks.

"The neatest thing happened today ... *(write about the coolest thing)*

_____
_____
_____
_____
_____
_____
_____

... so I called ... *(name the first person you would talk to about this)*

_____

and she/he said, *(write what he/she would say)*

_____
_____
_____
_____
_____
_____
_____

40.

How important is honesty to you?

Anger

41.

If you could wipe out all the bad moments in your life, would you? Why or why not?

42.

What is the most violent thing you have ever done to someone else? (Remember, violent acts are not always physical acts.) Why? Describe your feelings about your own violence.

43.

Draw a picture of a person you really dislike. Why do you dislike this person so much?

44.
Is it ever a good thing to get angry?

45.

Draw yourself when you are angry. Write the kind of things you say (out loud and inside your head) when you are mad.

Boundaries

46.

What object or person do you respect most in the world and why?

47.
If you were president of the United States, what are some things you would change, if you could?

48.

If trust looked like something, what would it look like? How important is trust to you?

49.
What are the things you would never, ever let anyone do to you?

50.

**What's one rule in your home or at
school that you would change?
Write a letter to your parent
or to a teacher explaining this issue,
and suggest what you would like
to see happen.**

Saying No

51.

Describe a time you wanted to say no but didn't. Would you say something different if you had to do it all over again? What would you do?

52.

Write down the word NO in big letters in the middle of your page. Then, all around the word, write down all the people and things you have ever wanted to say no to.

53.

Write a story that begins, "Once upon a time, there was a little girl who said no to everything." What happens?

54.
Write "I deserve to be listened to because ..." and then write ten characteristics about yourself you really like and admire.

55.

Name three times you said yes and were glad you did.

Me, Special Me

56.

Write down the nicest thing anyone has ever said to you. How did you feel when you heard this?

57.

Imagine your mother and your grandmother sit down and have a conversation about who you are and what you've become. Write out that conversation.

58.

If you were a famous artist, what kind of art (music, dance, writing, painting) would you create?

59.
**If you could be reincarnated
and come back to life as any animal,
what animal would you choose?**

60.

**When your family gets together
and tells stories about you and other
people in the family (maybe ones you've
heard many times before),
what stories do they tell?**

Bibliography

Goldberg, Natalie. *Writing Down the Bones: Freeing the Writer Within.* Boston: Shambhala, 1986.

Metzger, Deena. *Writing for Your Life: A Guide and Companion to the Inner World.* United Kingdom: HarperCollins, 1992.

Progroff, Ira. *At a Journal Workshop: Writing to Access the Power of the Unconscious and Evoke Creative Ability.* New York: Dialogue House Library, 1989.

Try these additional resources.

EMPOWER ME!
12 Sessions for Building Self-Esteem in Girls

Helen Raica-Klotz

Paper, 64 pages, 8½" x 11", ISBN: 0-89390-448-1

Empower Me! 12 Sessions for Building Self-Esteem in Girls is the training manual you should use with *Journal Me! A Pocketbook for Girls*. The first six sessions (Discover Me!) help girls explore their individuality. The second set of six sessions ("Me and Others") helps girls improve their relationships with family and friends. Because of the powerful nature of the *Empower Me!* exercises, facilitators should either be professional counselors themselves or collaborate with one.

THE SERVICE VOLUNTEER'S HANDBOOK

Ret Thomas and Dorine Thomas

Paperbound, 96 pages, 4¼" x 7", ISBN: 0-89390-442-2

The Service Volunteer's Handbook is the perfect tool to put into your service learners' hands before they go out into the field. This little book — it even fits in a pocket planner — tells students how to get organized for service, what their roles and responsibilities are, how to behave in a helping environment, how to maintain good relationships, and how to keep a positive perspective. The second half of the book covers basic skills important to service volunteers. Back pages includes client profile sheets and an address book.

Order these books from your local bookseller or call: CODE: JM
1-888-273-7782 (toll free) or 1-408-286-8505
or visit the web site at www.rpinet.com